Joe Satriani
GUITAR SECRETS

**41 PRIVATE LESSONS
AS FEATURED IN**

guitar

—— **INCLUDES** ——
**chords • scales & modes • tunings
theory • technique • harmonics • soloing**

To access audio visit:
www.halleonard.com/mylibrary

5520-1362-7090-5673

Foreword

Few guitarists in the history of the instrument have had the far-reaching influence of Joe Satriani. To music lovers he is revered as one of the great rock guitar instrumentalists of our time. But to guitarists throughout the world he is a fountain of both inspiration and information. His wealth of musical knowledge and innate ability to share it have taken on another level of wonder as Joe's students have gone out on their own to create some of the most unique and celebrated guitar sounds in rock. Kirk Hammett, Steve Vai and Alex Skolnick are among those students. Here is your chance to join them. It is my hope—and Joe's—that these lessons, which first appeared in *GUITAR For The Practicing Musician*, will inspire all who use them to achieve the creative heights to which they aspire.

— JOHN STIX
Editor-In-Chief
GUITAR For The Practicing Musician

INTRODUCTION

A few years ago, the editors of GUITAR For The Practicing Musician asked me to contribute to their "Guitar Secrets" column. I jumped at the opportunity.

Each month, a short, concise and thoroughly useful idea, with examples, would be presented so that the reader, within a few minutes, could gain useful information that was ready for application.

After three years and forty-one installments, we wound up with an impressive body of work covering an enormous amount of musical ground. Chords, scales, tunings, theory, whammy bar stuff, etc.... You name it, I covered it.

So we've put it all together in one book for all to explore and enjoy.

BEST of luck!

—JOE SATRIANI

CONTENTS

Advanced Improvising (May '90) 31
Advanced Improvising, Revisited (Oct. '90) 37
Atonal Scat Singing (Mar. '88) 8

Chromatic Warm-Up (June '90) 33
Compound Octaves (Sept. '90) 23

Finding the Note (Nov. '87) 5
Flutter Power (Part One) (Jan. '89) 17
Flutter Power (Part Two) (Feb. '89) 18

Grouped Articulations (Mar. '89) 19
Grouped Articulations: Threes (Apr. '89) 20

Harmonic Crunch (Nov. '90) 38
Harmonized Minor Pentatonic (June '89) 22
Harmonized Scales (Part One) (Jan. '88) 7
Harmonized Scales (Part Two) (Feb. '88) 7
The Hindu Scale (Aug. '90) 35

Light and Funky Chords (Oct. '88) 15

Modal Arpeggios (Nov. '88) 15

Natural-Harmonic Map (Sept. '90) 36

Octaves (July '89) 22
One-String Scales (Apr. '88) 9
Open D Blues (Apr. '90) 30

Open Tuning (May '88) 10
Open-String Color (Dec. '90) 39

Photographic Memory (Part One) (Oct. '89) 24
Photographic Memory (Part Two) (Nov. '89) 25
Practical Ear Training (Aug. '89) 23

Re-Assigning Chord Intervals (Jan. '91) 39
Right-Hand Harmonics (Dec. '87) 6

Smart Fingers (Sept. '87) 4
Smart Fingers (Part Two) (May '89) 21
Soloing in All 12 Keys (Aug. '88) 13
Suspended Chords (Dec. '88) 16

Thrash Soloing (Part One) (Feb. '90) 28
Thrash Soloing (Part Two) (Mar. '90) 29
Triad Arpeggios (June '88) 10
Triads (Part One) (Dec. '89) 26
Triads (Part Two) (Jan. '90) 27
Twenty-One 4th-String-Root Chords (July '90) 34

Uncommon Arpeggios (Sept. '88) 14
Unusual Tunings (Oct. '87) 5

The Wang Bar (July '88) 12

Audio Track Listing 40

Recording Credits: Dave Celentano, Guitar
Management: Bill Graham Management
Edited by Andy Aledort, Bruce Pollock and Jon Chappell
Layout and Illustrations: Jon Chappell
Music Engraving by Gordon Hallberg
Cover Design: Brian Austin
Production Manager: Daniel Rosenbaum
Director of Music: Mark Phillips
Photography by Neil Zlozower

ISBN 978-1-60378-358-3

September '87: SMART FINGERS

Finger exercises can be helpful in many ways. They are not only good for warming up, but also for introducing new techniques into your vocabulary. Diversification is paramount. The more you know, the better. Here is an exercise I call "The Diminished Chord Relay." It involves playing seven diminished chords in rapid succession up and down the fretboard. It's a veritable finger-twister.

First memorize the chord voicings in Ex. 1. Strum #1 once, making sure it sounds good, with no buzzy noises and no open strings. Then with your strumming hand, mute the strings. While the strings are muted, finger chord #2. Once you have it, strum it just as you did the first chord. Move on to #3, #4, and then back to #3, #2 and finally #1, always using the same strum-mute-switch routine. After you've got that down, repeat the exercise a half step (one fret) higher. Be sure to maintain the same intervallic relationship between each of the chords and remember to start out slowly and develop coordination first. It's quality before speed every time.

For variation, try the approach as shown in Ex. 2. Arpeggiate each chord with muted strings. One picking style that works well in this situation is down-up-up-up.

The Diminished Chord Relay is an excellent exercise for developing "smart fingers," as long as it remains challenging to your technique. So when it becomes easy, make it difficult. If it gets boring, make it interesting. And don't forget to listen to the *sound* of the chords. Used creatively, diminished chords can do what no other chords can. Experiment, and find out what that is.

Ex. 1

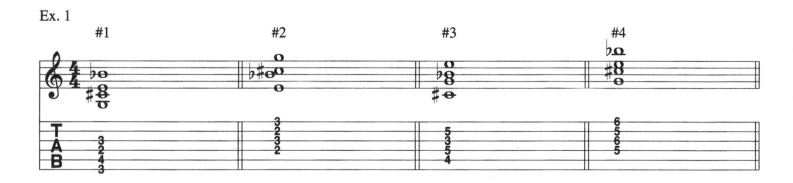

Ex. 2

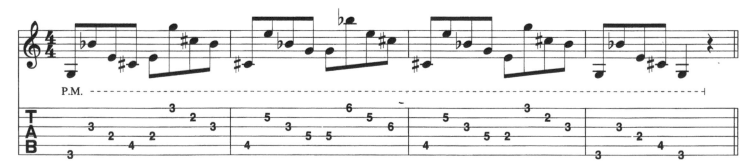

October '87: UNUSUAL TUNINGS

I have always considered the guitar's tuning flexibility to be one of its greatest attributes. This month I would like to show you how you can get some interesting results with some unusual tunings.

Let's start with the tuning I used for "Flow My Tears" on Stuart Hamm's debut album, *Radio Free Albymuth*. The song is in the key of E minor, with the chords and melody spelling out an Em9 to Cmaj9#11 pattern. The drifting quality of the piece inspired me to play harmonics in a random pattern supporting both melody and harmony. Here is the tuning I used (bottom to top): E G D G A D.

By playing harmonics on the 5th, 7th and 12th frets, I was able to produce notes sympathetic to the changes, as well as create a combination bell/kalimba-like sound. With the application of dynamics, you will find the timbre of these harmonics can vary. That's something I would like you to experiment with. I used this tuning and technique together, with a variation, for "Rubina," found on my *Not of This Earth* release. The variation: E G D E A E.

"Rubina" and "Flow My Tears" are in the relative keys G major and E minor, respectively—thus the compatibility of the tunings and songs. Try playing the harmonics in groups of two—two harmonics at once—jumping positions and skipping strings, to create a kalimba-like sound. For a more cascading harmonic bell sound, pick each harmonic separately while applying a simple or complex rhythm. With some reverb, delay or stereo chorus—or a combination of all three—you will find you can create a truly sublime sound. Tune up and explore.

November '87: FINDING THE NOTE

It is important to know your way around your instrument, and through the years I have seen many fretboard exercises developed for just this purpose. Some of them are easy, some are difficult; some of them a lot of fun, some unbearable. Finding one that works can be rough. But here is one that does, provided you play by my rules. You will need a guitar, a metronome, and a good dose of concentration.

Decide on a note you wish to locate and set your metronome to 60. Then with each click of the metronome, locate that note on the 6th string in all positions. Without missing a beat, proceed to the 5th string and find that note, again, in every possible position. Play on the beat, continue on all strings and use the open-string positions too. Remember, NO CHEATING. If 60 is too fast, slow it down. If it is too slow, speed it up. And most important, practice with all 12 notes.

If you are just starting out, find a note chart (a graphic representation of the fretboard showing the names of the notes and where they are found). Use it to help in finding the desired notes. Do this exercise every day until you are so good at it you can do it in your sleep.

December '87: Right-Hand Harmonics

This technique is one of my favorites. I find it helps in making notes sound more expressive and lively. It also facilitates octave displacement as well as large-interval hopping. Let's begin by bending your 1st finger to play C on the G string (5th fret). Make sure your thumb is grabbing the neck. The side of your knuckle on the 1st finger should be flush with the side of the neck at about the 3rd fret. Using a downward pulling motion of the wrist, bend the G string one whole step higher to D. Repeat this a few times, making sure your intonation is good.

Now that I've got you bending on the fretboard, use your picking hand to downpick the G string about 4½ inches from the bridge, allowing a bit of your right-hand thumb to touch the string along with the pick. This will give you the same two notes two octaves higher. When picking 3½ inches from the bridge, you will get notes a major 3rd higher than that, and at 3 inches a perfect 5th higher. At 2¾ inches you get a minor 7th higher and at 2½ inches you will hear the third octave. With each different fret position your harmonic positions change. So play around the neck to get a feel for these ever-changing positions.

This technique will work on every string, some better than others. And as far as the left hand goes, you can pull up or down a minor 2nd, a major 2nd, a minor 3rd, a major 3rd or as far as you can manage. Good luck and have fun.

January '88: HARMONIZED SCALES (PART ONE)

Here's a lesson I enjoy giving because the benefits and possibilities are great, while the method is simple and easy to implement. I'm talking about harmonized scales. Let's get specific. If you stay within the bounds of the major scale you will find that each note can be harmonized with one or more notes from the same scale, with varying results. Let's try a two-octave C major scale harmonized in 3rds (see Staff 1). As you can see, we get major 3rds for the notes C, F and G (root, 4th and 5th), and minor 3rds for the notes D, E, A and B (2nd, 3rd, 6th and 7th). Next try the A minor scale in three octaves (see Staff 2).

I think you will find practicing in three or more octaves more beneficial with exercises of this nature. Remember, it is essential that you try to memorize every fingering and positional variation in all keys. We all know that exercises are not well known for their "musical swing," so you will have to take this concept and apply it to an actual melody, solo or support line to really hear it work. Thirds have a very harmonious sound, but there are many other options when considering harmonization. Next month we will explore some other options.

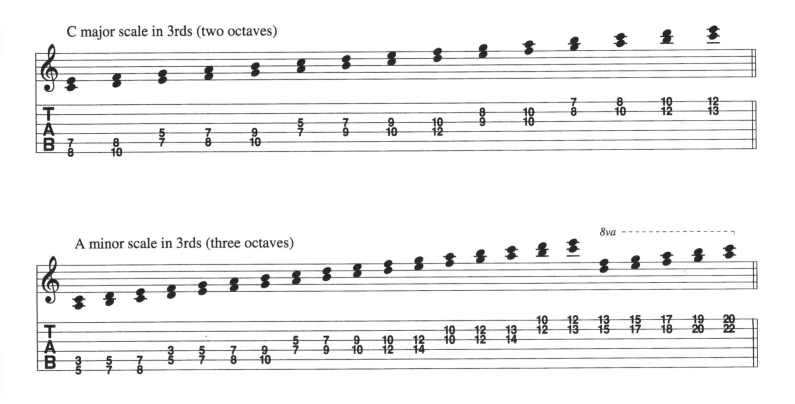

February '88: HARMONIZED SCALES (PART TWO)

Last month I discussed the techniques and benefits of learning scales harmonized in 3rds in both two and three octaves. Let's move on to 4ths and 5ths. Using the G major scale, we find that it takes a variety of 4ths and 5ths to set up the correct harmony (see Staves 1 and 2). Once memorized, transpose into all keys. Play slowly and pay close attention to the characteristics of these harmonies. By that I mean their uniqueness and their "color." Each interval has its own sound, and knowing these sounds will put you in control. Next, try writing a melody or solo and harmonize it using 3rds, 4ths and 5ths in any combination you like. Experiment.

Harmonized guitar lines are very popular these days. For the most outrageous example, I recommend Steve Vai's "The Attitude Song" (transcribed in the Nov. '87 issue of *GUITAR For The Practicing Musician*). Steve puts more guitar harmonies per vinyl inch in that song than anything else I have ever heard. For something completely different, try "New Day" on my *Not of This Earth* Lp or "Circles" on my latest release, *Surfing with the Alien*. Listen. Enjoy. Learn. Experiment.

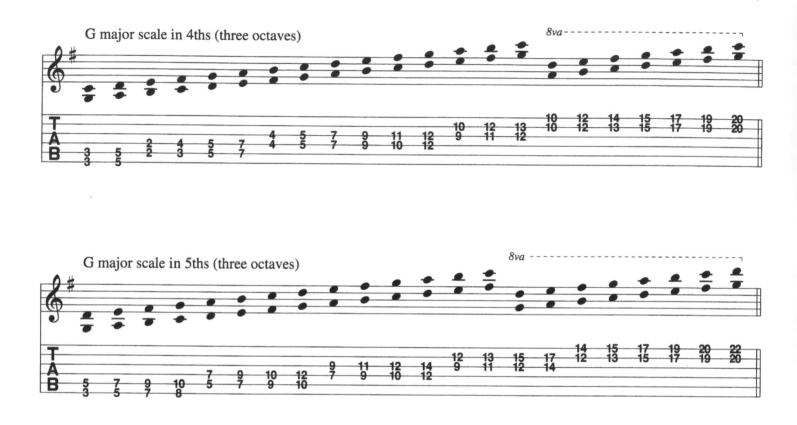

March '88: ATONAL SCAT SINGING

With a title like "Atonal Scat Singing," you can be sure this is not going to be your average Guitar Secrets installment. This time I want to show you a perplexing ear-training endurance exercise that will bring together the imagination, the mind and the instrument. This exercise comes to us courtesy of Lennie Tristano, "The Father of Cool Jazz," the brilliant pianist-composer who bopped with the best. He taught his students to memorize everything, to embrace discipline, and above all, to play only what you *want* to play. I was once a student of Lennie Tristano's and I will never forget the experience.

For the exercise, set the metronome to 60. Using eighth notes, play randomly anywhere and everywhere on the fretboard. Use downstrokes. You must keep this up without stopping for approximately three minutes. As you play try to anticipate what each note will sound like. Do not play clichés or familiar patterns. Think and play in free-form. No style, just notes. When you pass the three-minute mark, start singing the notes you are playing. You can use any one-syllable sound you like. Keep this up for a few minutes or until you cannot continue further. This exercise is a strange and beautiful thing. I'm consistently impressed with how it always makes me feel closer to the sound of music.

Thank you, Lennie Tristano.

April '88: One-String Scales

Changing the way you think about music can help you get out of old habits and break new ground. For the modern guitarist, one-string scales are a must. From two-handed lines and arpeggios to sweeping legato runs, these patterns are some of the most widely used today. They can also help you see scales in a different way, as if they were straight lines. Yes, I think linear. In Ex. 1 I have written the patterns in groups of three. Play them as written, with down-up-down-up picking. Accent the first of every three notes.

For variation try Ex. 2. Where the first two patterns are built for speed, these two will force you to see the scale as a straight line. Once you have memorized theses scales, apply this concept to the scales you use the most often. Use different rhythms and picking techniques for variation. Your goals should include memorizing all scales in all keys. Remember: knowledge is power.

Ex. 1

F major

C Dorian

Ex. 2

E harmonic minor

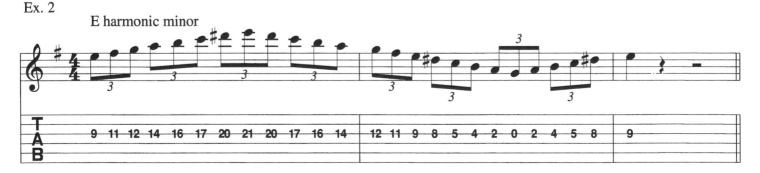

D Phrygian dominant

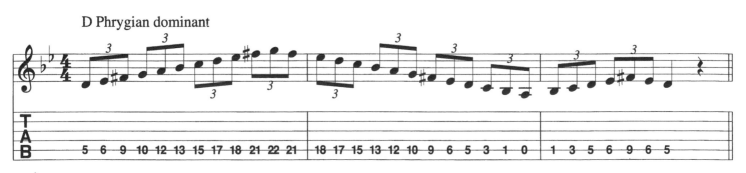

May '88: Open Tuning

Take your guitar and tune the 6th string down one whole step. Next, bring the 5th string down to G. Leave strings 4, 3, and 2 as they are (D, G and B, respectively). Finally, take the 1st string down one whole step to D. There you have the open G tuning (see Ex. 1).

This type of tuning not only sounds great but offers a "guitar rhythm" approach not possible with standard tuning. For the last 25 years Keith Richards has proved it with "19th Nervous Breakdown," "Gimme Shelter," "Brown Sugar," "Can't You Hear Me Knockin'" and "Start Me Up," to name a few. For simple ideas that sound big, try those in Ex. 2.

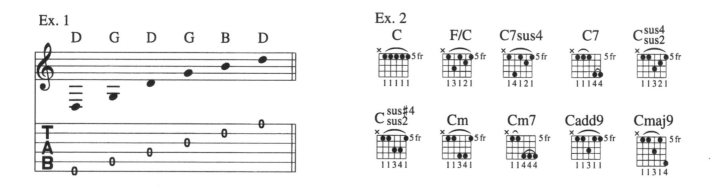

Mix these up a bit and apply some rhythm. I am sure you will find some good patterns taking shape. Take note that since no open strings are used with these chords, they are movable. In other words, MOVE 'EM AROUND! Any style of music is possible with this or any other open tuning, from ancient folk music to the unique music of Adrian Belew (check out "Ballet for the Blue Whale" on his *Twang Bar King* Lp). So experiment and keep an open mind. There is a good book of chords and tunings that is a must for those of you who wish to know more. It's called *Chords and Tunings for Fretted Instruments* by Larry Sandberg (Oak Publications). Find it. Read it. Learn it. And have some fun with the guitar.

June '88: Triad Arpeggios

Here is a triad arpeggio exercise that spans 13 frets and uses all six strings. It is an excellent workout for both hands and it will help you visualize more clearly how a chord can be spread out over the fretboard. Written are the triads F major (1, 3, 5), F minor (1, ♭3, 5), F diminished (1, ♭3, ♭5), F augmented (1, 3, ♯5) and Fsus4 (1, 4, 5). Play them with alternating strokes.

These arpeggios should be practiced in all positions. Following a cycle of 4ths can be useful here. Play each of the five arpeggios off the following notes (in the order written): C, F, B♭, E♭, A♭, D♭, G♭, B, E, A, D, G. If you cannot complete an arpeggio due to lack of frets, simply go as far as your fretboard permits.

This exercise should be practiced with a metronome at a comfortable tempo. Coordination first. Then speed. Good luck!

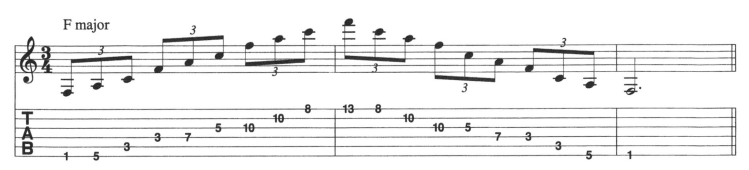

F major

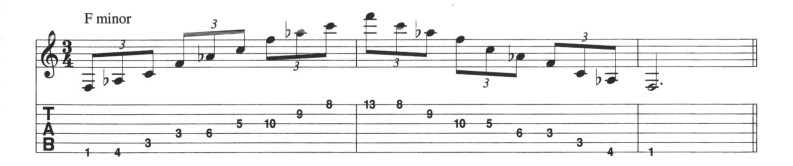

F minor

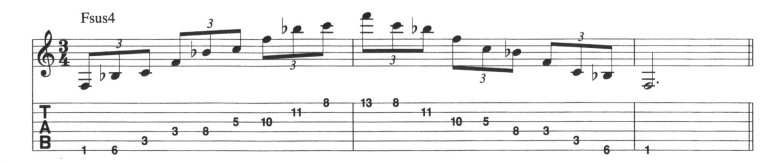

F diminished

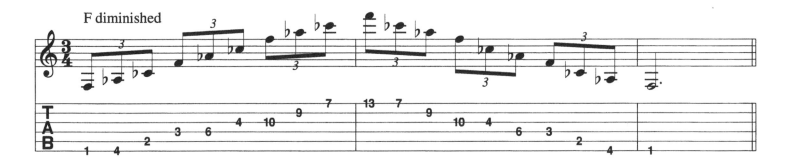

F augmented

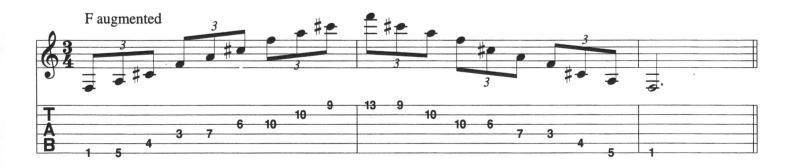

Fsus4

July '88: THE WANG BAR

Some people like to wang, some people don't. Some people wang all the time, some just a little. Any way you look at it, wanging is big business these days. And everybody's looking for the NEW WANG. Or at least a new way to wang. So here is my contribution to fellow wangers out there in Wangdom.

WANG #1: You'll need a guitar with a wang bar, an amp with a generous amount of distortion, and a pick. You will also need to be familiar with the technique of creating harmonics with the right-hand thumb. This is accomplished by allowing a bit of your right-hand thumb to touch the string or strings as they are picked. Start with a broad downstroke across strings 4, 3 and 2, about four inches from the bridge. Use the right-hand thumb technique to create two or three harmonics. Simultaneously, reach over with your left hand, grab the bar, and swiftly but smoothly bringing it down, then up as far as you can. Hold it for a brief moment, then quickly bring it down until the strings fret out. This should take about four seconds.

WANG #2: With the same setup, strike A♭ on the 3rd string, 1st fret, and slowly slide it all the way up the neck. It should take about one second. Simultaneously and slowly, push the bar down in an effort to maintain the warbling pitch of the string. After you get the hand of it, try doing it faster and in groups of two or three for a more overt effect.

WANG #3: Carefully unscrew or disengage wang bar from guitar and put in case. Sometimes the best way to wang is not to wang at all.

August '88: SOLOING IN ALL 12 KEYS

A few years ago I wrote a piece of music called "Endless Rain." My idea was to create a chord progression using all 12 natural minor keys that could be used in teaching students how to solo off each chromatic tone. The results were phenomenal. Soon I had students cutting up the entire fretboard with searing melodies and blazing solos. Now it's your turn. But before you tackle the solo, you must embrace the rhythm. Because of this, some of my students changed the title to "Endless Pain." Now you will see why. The changes are in Ex. 1. The chord voicings in Ex. 2 may help. You can play the chords as sustained sixteenth-note arpeggios if you like (see Ex. 3). Each two-bar pattern starting with the madd9 chord should be treated as a two-bar Aeolian or minor scale phrase. The root of the minor chord is the root of the scale. There are ways to bend the rules and make some "wrong" notes "right" here. But for now, work with the minor scale and conquer it.

Ex. 1

‖: Bmadd9	Gadd9	Emadd9	Cadd9	
Amadd9	Fadd9	Dmadd9	B♭add9	
Gmadd9	E♭add9	Cmadd9	A♭add9	
Fmadd9	D♭add9	B♭madd9	G♭add9	
E♭madd9	Badd9	G♯madd9	Eadd9	
C♯madd9	Aadd9	F♯madd9	Dadd9	:‖

Ex. 2

Ex. 3

September '88: UNCOMMON ARPEGGIOS

The playing of a chord with its notes sounded in succession, rather than simultaneously, is the standard definition of an arpeggio. Some use the term "broken chord." Whatever you call it, it is a good idea and a useful tool in making music interesting. And that is the idea.

The definition also implies that any chord can be arpeggiated. So let's skip the mundane and try something uncommon. Chords such as m11, maj9#11, sus4-sus2, 11 and 11♭9 produce some interesting results. Use alternating strokes and play ascending and descending in all keys.

You will have to be relaxed and ready if you want to speed through these. They may be difficult at first but don't give up; it always takes time. Meanwhile, let me put this in your ear. Next time you are playing in a Dorian or Aeolian mode, try using arpeggios #1 and #3 off the root. When in a Lydian mode, arpeggio #2 will add an interesting touch. Arpeggios #3 and #4 will work with the Mixolydian mode. Reserve #5 for the Phrygian dominant mode. I trust you will use these with discretion and taste.

October '88: LIGHT AND FUNKY CHORDS

Some of the most effective rhythm guitar work is done with as few notes as possible—in other words, using voicings with two or three notes and concentrating on strings 1 through 4. Using these parameters you can get drop-dead funky like Prince ("Kiss" and "Sign of the Times") or big and beautiful like the Edge ("Pride" and "Wire").

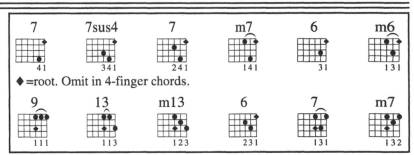

Learn the following chords up and down the fretboard. Some of these chords sound better in different octaves. So experiment. For a funky sound, play with a dry, clean tone and get your strumming hand moving down-up-down-up in a sixteenth-note pattern. With the left hand, use pressure and mute techniques to build a tight rhythmic pattern. Start slowly and build to the desired speed. For more spacial effects, allow these voicings to ring out over a driving rhythm. Some signal processing—reverb, chorus and/or delay—can be helpful. Bands like The Fixx and The Police have this type of approach. Keep an open mind and have fun.

November '88: MODAL ARPEGGIOS

If you take a mode and arrange its intervals like this—1, 3, 5, 7, 9, 11, 13—you get what I call a modal arpeggio. By arranging the scale this way and arpeggiating it, you can hear the harmonic sequence of the notes as if they were a seven-note chord. For example, the major scale spelled out above will sound like a I chord competing with its V7 chord. However, with the Lydian, Mixolydian, Dorian and Lydian dominant modes, the results are very interesting. Each note complements the others. I've written these out in D, with the root on the 5th string. But they should be learned everywhere they can be played. With a good measure of style and taste these arpeggios can be very useful and lots of fun.

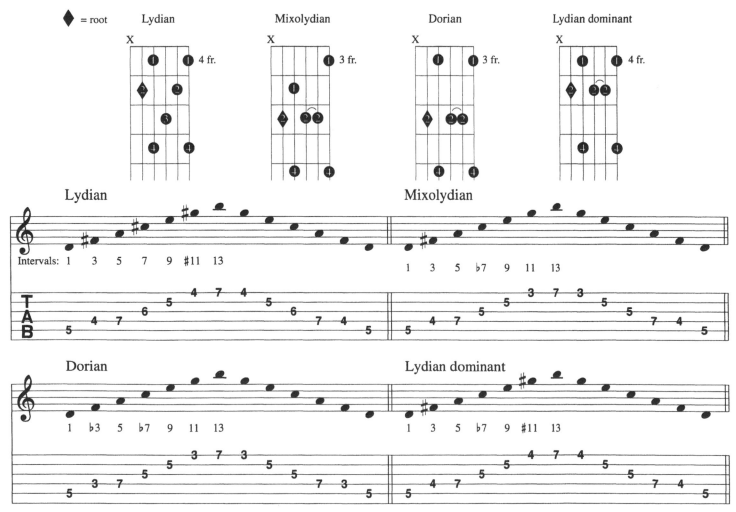

15

December '88: SUSPENDED CHORDS

A sus2 chord is a triad whose 3rd is replaced with a major 2nd, thus creating the voicing 1, 2, 5. This can sound similar to an Aadd9 chord (1, 3, 5, 9), but it is a truly different chord, with a unique voice function. And technically it must be expressed as a sus2 because no 3rd is present. Over the years I've heard these eight fingerings used by Jimi Hendrix, Jimmy Page, Andy Summers, Prince, the Edge, Keith Richards, Adrian Belew, John Abercrombie, Eddie Van Halen and Steve Vai with great results: "Little Wing," "Hina," "Midnight Rambler," "Message in a Bottle," "Purple Rain" and "Ramble On," to name a few.

Get to know these chords. Move them around the fretboard and make some music. I'm sure you will find them attractive. Some of the best players already have!

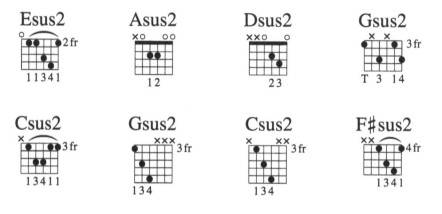

16

January '89: FLUTTER POWER (PART ONE)

This month I want to work on your flutter power. That's right. It's time to put some punch in those fluttery embellishments some of you may know as trills, mordents and turns. The trill is an ornament consisting of the rapid alternation of a note with the one next to it, or with any other note for that matter. And it is this embellishment I wish to focus on specifically.

Trills date back to the 13th century and have been widely used to this date. Jimi Hendrix used them quite a bit to get a fluttery sound out of long single-string runs, and I think this technique could greatly enhance your playing.

Let's get down to basics with a chromatic exercise. Follow the manuscript/tab shown (three bars). Pick only the first note in each measure. Hammer on and pull off the remaining notes.

Next: Repeat this exercise on the 2nd string, then the 3rd and so on. Use the correct fingering as indicated. Playing along with a metronome will help you stay in time, and that's important with this exercise. Stay relaxed and don't overdo it.

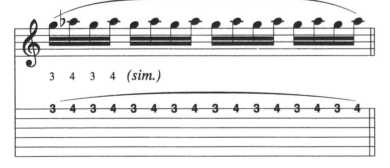

February '89: FLUTTER POWER (PART TWO)

Last month we discussed the trill, and I showed you a chromatic exercise to strengthen your fluttering technique. This month I would like to teach you two diatonic fluttering exercises. The first one is in the key of C major. The second exercise is in the key of A minor, and consists of a series of trills on one string. This fluttering technique can be applied to almost any melodic line or sequence, so I hope you will take these examples as cues to explore the possibilities. Proceed directly to the manuscript/tab. Stay in time. Use the suggested fingering. Stay loose.

March '89: GROUPED ARTICULATIONS

In Ex. 1 I've written a D minor pentatonic scale fingering. Once you get this wired, you'll find you can play it much faster than you could ever pick it. Ex. 2 is a sequence from the scale. The sequence is in groups of four. It begins with the 1st through 4th scale tones, then the 2nd through 5th, then the 3rd through 6th, etc. Once you master this, try groups of five (D to C, F to D, G to E, etc.) and then groups of six. And, of course, learn everything in reverse as well. You'll probably find reversing these a little more difficult physically, because it's easier to hammer on in the ascent than to pull off in the descent.

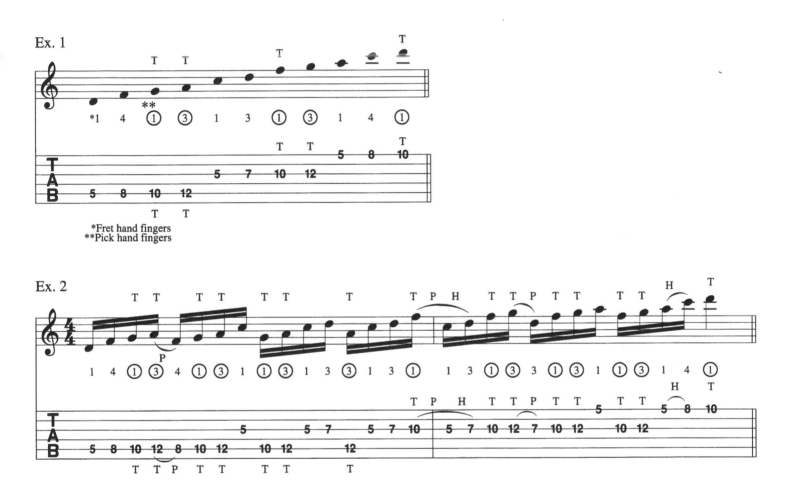

*Fret hand fingers
**Pick hand fingers

April '89: GROUPED ARTICULATIONS: THREES

Dear Students:

How are those articulated groups of two going? I hope all is well, 'cause we're movin' on to threes. This exercise will definitely improve your ability to stretch and connect with a high degree of articulation. The key element here is playing each group of triplet eighth notes on one string. Use triplet picking (down-up-down, down-up-down) or alternating strokes. This exercise will also work wonders on your ability to visualize scales on the fretboard. Start slowly and build speed with quality.

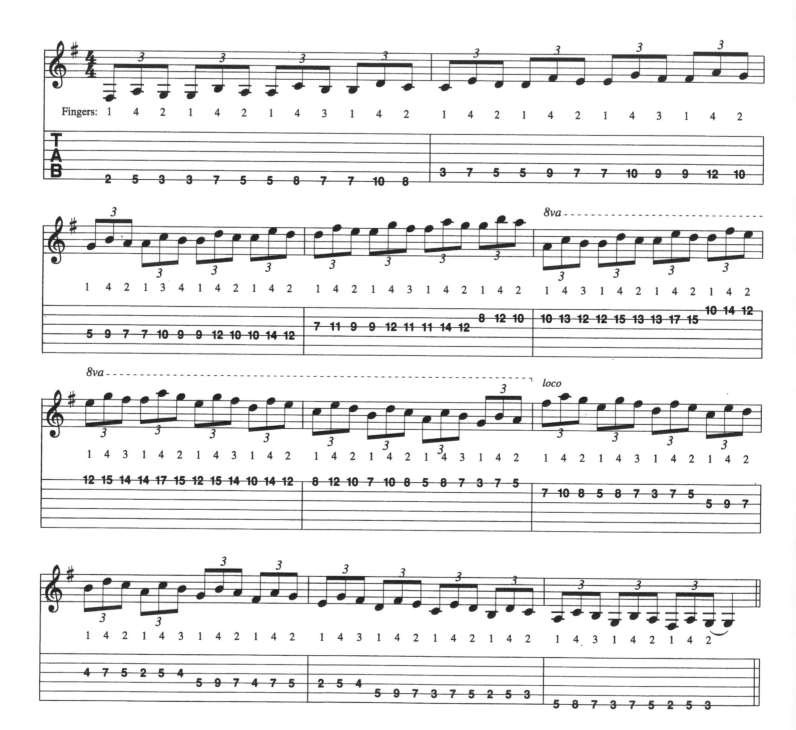

May '89: SMART FINGERS (PART TWO)

The exercises that follow are a product of my determination to develop a group of warm-up routines that are both effective and challenging. In my first Smart Fingers article (Sept. '87) I showed you an exercise called Diminished Chord Relay; I hope you're still using it! These patterns are very beneficial in developing basic coordination skills, and as I stated before, diversification is paramount.

This month's exercise is called "Diagonal Chord Relay." Each group of six chords should be cleanly strummed, then performed one fret higher. Start at the 1st fret and work your way up the fretboard. I've also included a variation that should get your equal attention. In playing these patterns use this approach: strum, mute, switch; strum, mute, switch. This technique will eliminate unwanted string noise when switching from chord to chord. Stay in tune. Stay in control. Keep in touch.

Ex. 1

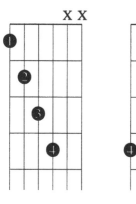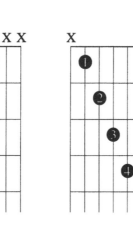

Ex. 2: Variation

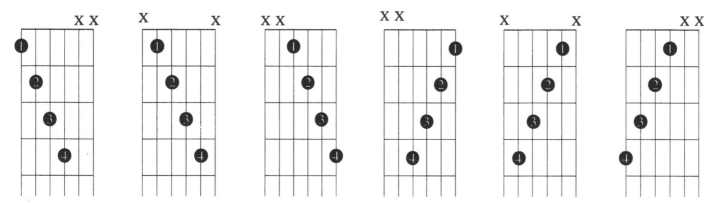

June '89: HARMONIZED MINOR PENTATONIC

The pentatonic scale consists of five pitches and can be termed "anhemitonic" because it does not contain semitones. This feature gives the pentatonic scale its open, tension-free sound. If we approach the scale harmonically, this "openness" becomes even more apparent. The pattern I present this month uses the A minor pentatonic scale, the intervals being: 1, ♭3, 4, 5, ♭7. By using 3rds and 4ths I've created a three-octave harmonized minor pentatonic pattern that is part exercise, part harmonic map and part study in tonality. Pay close attention to the uniqueness of this scale, and develop an opinion on possible applications. Eventually, it must be played and memorized in all keys. Good luck!

July '89: OCTAVES

The definition of an octave is an interval bounded by two pitches with the same pitch names, the higher of whose frequencies is twice the lower. More important, it's an attractive tool you can use to enhance your playing. From Wes Montgomery to Jimi Hendrix, George Benson to Steve Vai, almost every influential guitarist to date has used octaves to some degree. You should too! The following exercise should be treated as an introduction to octaves—how they sound, what they look like and where they can be found. I've used a three-octave G major scale as the parameter. Follow the music carefully and pay attention to the octave's sound. Then explore the possibilities.

August '89: PRACTICAL EAR TRAINING

The point of ear training is to improve musical perception. This means being able to recognize by ear: melodies, harmonies, intervals, rhythms, etc. I've used the word "practical" in this month's title because the exercise I'm going to show you is, well, practical. In other words, I've added a visual element that allows you to see the intervals in a one-octave scale format as you sing and play the notes.

The singing will help train your ears, while the seeing will introduce to you the positions of a scale's intervals. Sing each note you play—any syllable will do. At first, you can move the keys around to fit your vocal ability. Stay in pitch. Eventually, it must be learned in all keys. Work hard. Good luck!

September '89: COMPOUND OCTAVES

An octave is an interval bounded by two pitches with the same pitch names, the higher of whose frequencies is twice the lower. Here, I use the term *compound octaves* to indicate a third pitch an octave above the original or existing octave's higher pitch. The result: a three-note grouping of octaves. There are four fretted and movable fingerings shown, using the note B and its octaves. I have also included a B major scale pattern using a mix of these fingerings. Try arpeggiating each group with a pick, your thumb or any combination of your picking hand's thumb and fingers. If you wish to strum these octaves you will have to use a mute technique. Carefully cradle and mute the strings you do not wish to ring with your fretting hand's fingers, while fretting the desired notes. This will take practice. Take your time and concentrate on execution. Memorize this lesson in all keys, and feel free to blend, mix and match the fingerings shown. Good luck!

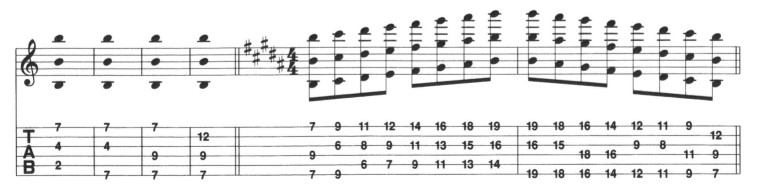

October '89: PHOTOGRAPHIC MEMORY (PART ONE)

This month I would like to show you a no-nonsense method for overcoming fretboard visualization problems with modes. The following example is comprised of seven one-position, two-octave scale forms. I've illustrated them using fretboard diagrams instead of manuscript because I want you to try to develop a photographic memory of these patterns. This is a pitch-axis type example and so I would like you to play each of these modes in diatonic order, off one root. Example: G major, G Dorian, G Phrygian, etc. Play each mode ascending and descending, without stopping at the higher octave. Rhythmically, you can use any pattern you like. The same goes for picking. Note the fingering: With these one-position scales, each finger is assigned a fret with the 1st finger taking care of two frets in some cases. Roots are circled. Work this out in all keys. Quality practice equals results. Good luck! Next month we'll do this example in three octaves.

◆ = root

Ionian/major

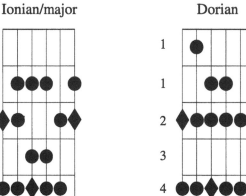

Dorian

Phrygian

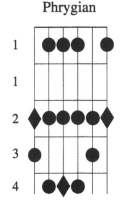

Lydian

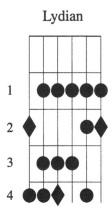

Mixolydian

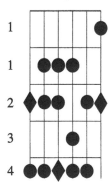

Aeolian/minor

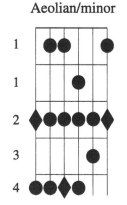

Locrian

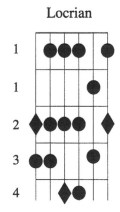

November '89: PHOTOGRAPHIC MEMORY (PART TWO)

This month I will show you an example that involves the playing of seven diatonic modes consecutively, in three octaves, using the pitch-axis method (off one root). As with last month's lesson, I will use fretboard diagrams for the purpose of helping you develop a photographic memory of these modal patterns. Play the scales, in the diatonic order shown, off one root, ascending and descending, without stopping. The fingering approach varies a bit on purpose: I want to keep you on your toes! Note the 1st-finger slides, a very good way to get around. Start slowly and build with confidence. You can experiment with rhythmic and articulation ideas, as long as you focus on the memorization of the scale's location on the fretboard. All roots are diamonds. As always, work in all keys. Best of luck!

◆ – root

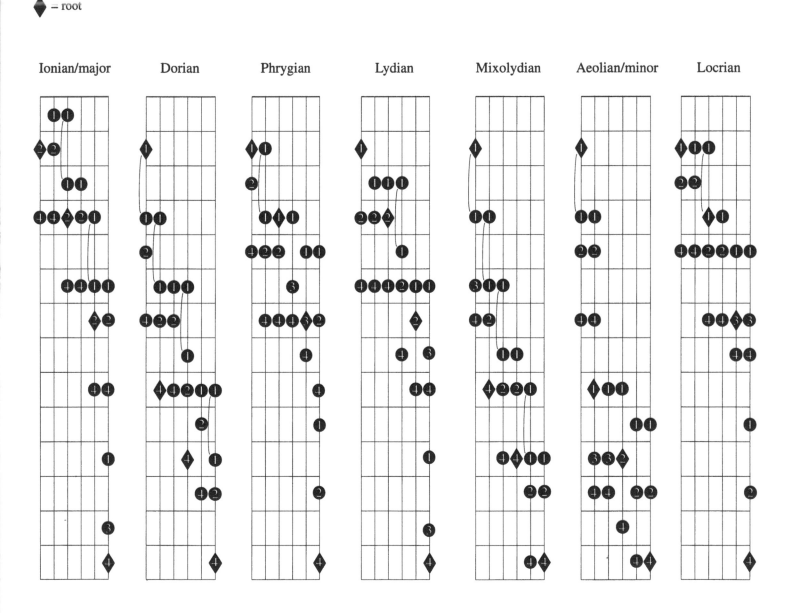

Ionian/major   Dorian   Phrygian   Lydian   Mixolydian   Aeolian/minor   Locrian

December '89: TRIADS (PART ONE)

Everybody's always talkin' 'bout triads! Why? Because the triad makes the Western music world go 'round. In lessons past I showed you two-octave and three-octave triad arpeggio exercises. This time we will approach the triads harmonically, playing them as three-note chords on adjacent strings up and down the neck. These are the harmonies: major (1, 3, 5), minor (1, ♭3, 5), diminished (1, ♭3, ♭5) and augmented (1, 3, ♯5).

Be neat, be clean, and memorize everything—in all keys.

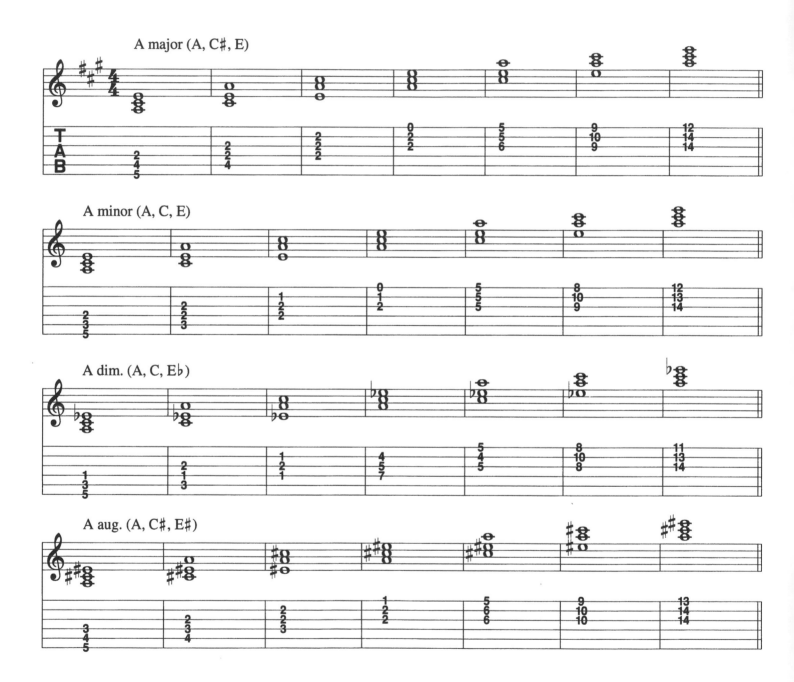

January '90: Triads (Part Two)

Welcome back to the land of the triad. This month we will finish up our harmonic triad study with three useful and unique chord forms: maj♭5 (1, 3, ♭5), sus4 (1, 4, 5) and sus2 (1, 2, 5). Most often these chords are used for tension, and resolve to major or minor chords. But that's not a rule, and exceptions are well in number. In fact, there are plenty of songs that use these chords as the basis of their composition and tonal center. I've written a few myself ("Not of This Earth," "Memories" and "Ice 9"). Play them. Memorize them. Divide and multiply.

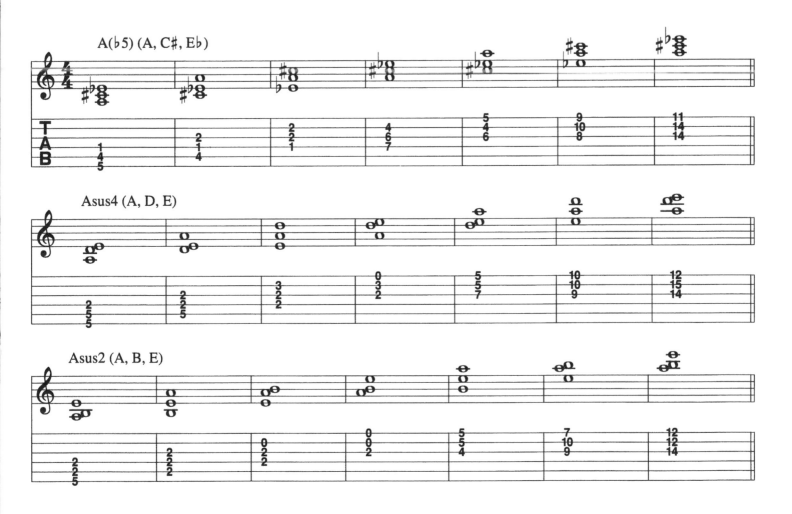

February '90: THRASH SOLOING (PART ONE)

Thrash metal progressions and chord patterns are often complex and difficult to solo over. They contain a large number of modulations, key changes and temporary tonal-center shifts. Add to that a drop-dead, hyper-crunch rhythm, and you've got your work cut out for you! If you're a fan of Metallica, Exodus, Testament, etc., then you've heard the soloists in these bands playing more than the usual minor pentatonic scale. They draw on a wide vocabulary of scales and modes to create their solos. This month we will use a very simple two-chord thrash pattern, and explore the sometimes exotic possibilities. I would like you to get to know the following scales:

Lydian: 1, 2, 3, #4, 5, 6, 7
Dorian#4:   1, 2, b3, #4, 5, 6, b7
Hungarian: 1, b2, 3, #4, 5, 6, b7
Symmetrical: 1, b2, b3, 3, #4, 5, 6, b7

They all work over this month's chord pattern, but the effect of each is quite different. So here they are in two-octave fingerings. Next month I will expand them to three octaves.

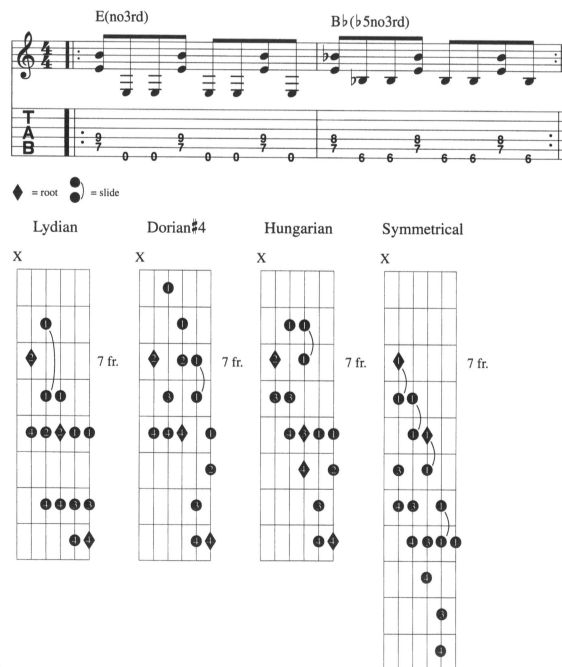

March '90: THRASH SOLOING (PART TWO)

This month we continue with our two-chord thrash pattern, and expand the four scale options to three octaves. Again, the E to B♭ chord progression presents us with some problems—or options—depending on how you look at it. Be creative. Be Different. Experiment!

Take note: There are some simple connections here that you can use to help in memorizing these scales. For example, E Lydian is the same as B major, C♯ Dorian, D♯ Phrygian, F♯ Mixolydian, G♯ minor and A♯ Locrian. Basically, for every note in a scale, there are that many modes or variations of the scale. Awesome! (See Guitar Secrets, Sept. and Oct. '89 for more two- and three-octave fingerings of these scales.) Again, the scale options are:

Lydian: 1, 2, 3, ♯4, 5, 6, 7
Dorian♯4:   1, 2, ♭3, ♯4, 5, 6, ♭7
Hungarian: 1, ♭2, 3, ♯4, 5, 6, ♭7
Symmetrical: 1, ♭2, ♭3, 3, ♯4, 5, 6, ♭7

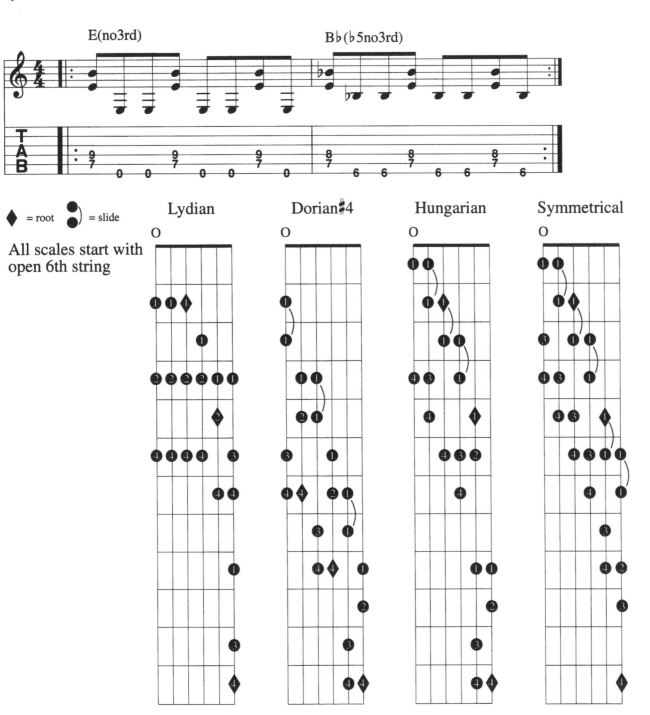

April '90: Open D Blues

Open D tuning is easy to learn and fun to play around with. It requires dropping string 6 to D, string 3 to F♯, string 2 to A, and string 1 to D. This gives you a D major chord when all six strings are played open. This is the voicing: D A D F♯ A D (1, 5, 1, 3, 5, 1). I've written out a few chord forms to be used with the blues pattern that follows. Use a slow to medium right-hand shuffle rhythm, two strums per chord. Using all downstrokes is a good way to get started, but feel free to improvise the rhythm.

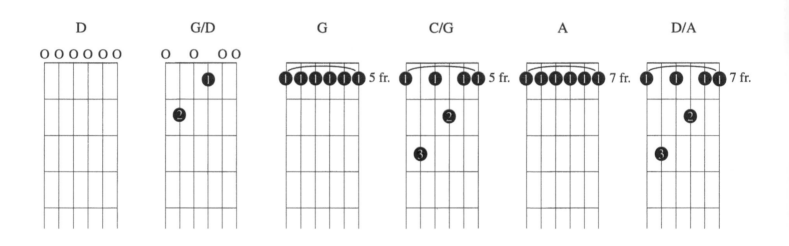

Shuffle rhythm

May '90: Advanced Improvising

I'm not going to give you a long speech on how to improvise, I'm just going to give you the space and framework to try it yourself. What follows is an excerpt from one of my unreleased instrumentals, called "The Eight Steps." It's a good progression to test your improvising skills as well as your ability to blend two- and three-octave scale forms around the fretboard. The scales used are: E Lydian, G Lydian, B Lydian, E Dorian and B minor (these last two scales are related to each other, as well as to G Lydian—see manuscript). Follow the scale suggestions written for each two-bar phrase. You can check my Guitar Secrets for Oct. and Nov. '89 (Photographic Memory, Parts One and Two) for complete two- and three-octave scale forms.

Each chord should be freely arpeggiated, allowing the notes to sustain in harmony. The most important thing to remember, though, is to make music. Use the scale/modes to create the kind of solo *you* like. Good luck.

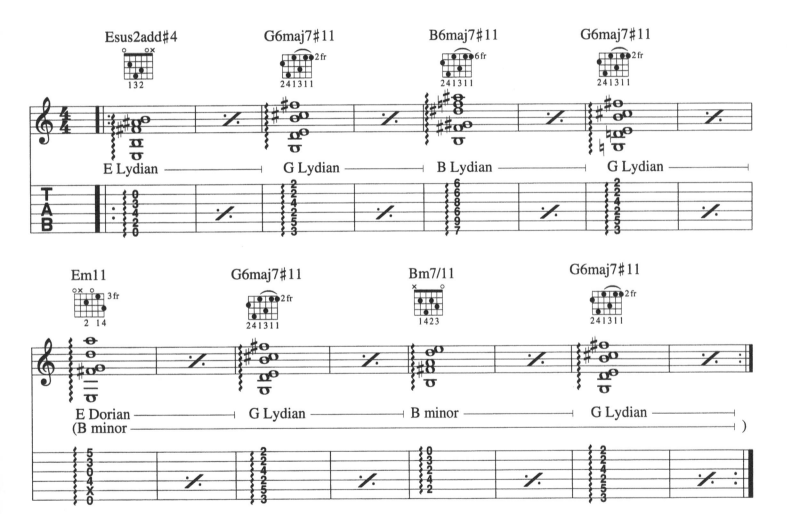

(continued on next page)

(*Advanced Improvising continued*)

Scale patterns used for "The Eight Steps"

♦ = root

🌑) = slide

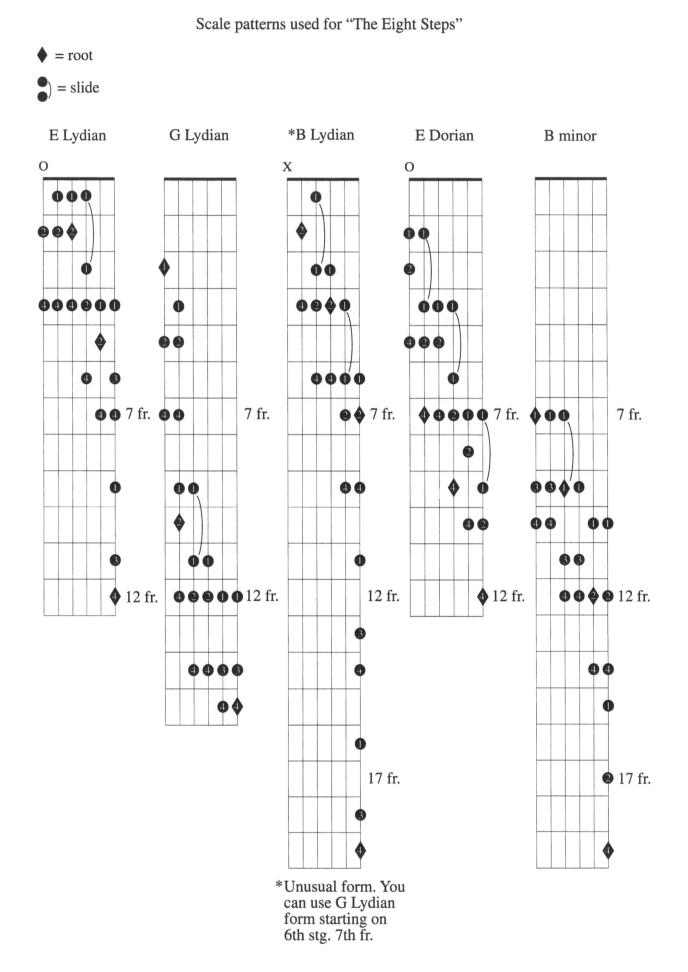

*Unusual form. You
 can use G Lydian
 form starting on
 6th stg. 7th fr.

June '90: CHROMATIC WARM-UP

As a teacher, there have been times when the tables turned and I learned a thing or two from my students. Case in point: Here is a good warm-up exercise that Steve Vai, after learning it from someone else, passed on to me. It will work wonders for your picking technique. Just start off slowly, pay attention to detail, and keep your hands, wrists and forearms relaxed. Tension will work against your coordination and eventually slow you down, so take it easy and do it right.

The exercise is written starting on the 1st fret, but it can be initiated anywhere on the fretboard. However, when starting on the 1st fret, the tablature's numbers are the same as the required fingering. Example: 1st finger is used for all notes on the 1st fret; 2nd finger used for all notes on the 2nd fret, etc. Use alternating strokes. I think the tab and manuscript will fill you in on everything else you need to know about this exercise, so give it all you can! Good luck!

July '90: TWENTY-ONE 4TH-STRING-ROOT CHORDS

Knowing "all the chords" is all-important in my book. Think of chord knowledge as harmonic freedom: The more you know, the more options you have. So this month I want to increase your harmonic vocabulary with 21 chords that use the 4th string as the root. All chords use strings 1, 2, 3 and 4, and are written as A chords. (If you wish to add the open 5th string for some bass support, go right ahead.) Strum each chord however you wish, but keep in mind that you're trying to memorize the sound as well as the name and fingering of each chord. As always, these "movable" chords should be memorized in all keys. Play on!

Twenty-one 4th-string-root chords

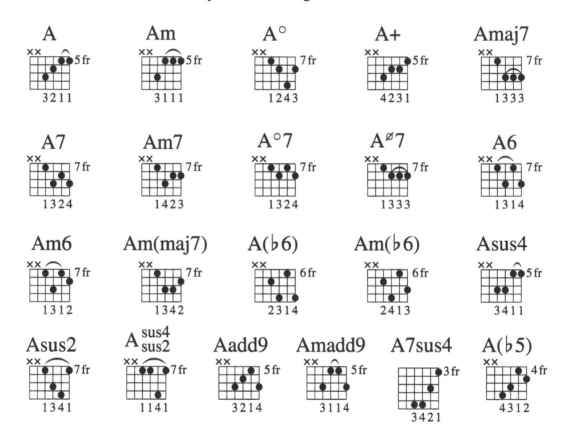

August '90: THE HINDU SCALE

I will now unravel for you the mystery of the Hindu scale: 1, 2, 3, 4, 5, ♭6, ♭7. That's not too hard to grasp, now is it? In fact, the Hindu scale could also be called the Aeolian dominant mode, the fifth mode of the Ascending melodic minor scale (1, 2, ♭3, 4, 5, 6, 7). Enough with the formula stuff! This month's lesson is to be a casual introduction to the Hindu scale complete with three scale fingerings and a short compositional example in progression form. Learn it and play it over and over until you get comfortable with it. Then try to come up with a variation of your own. Check out Led Zep's "Ten Years Gone" on the *Physical Graffiti* album; the quiet verses use the Hindu scale. Those guys were so clever!

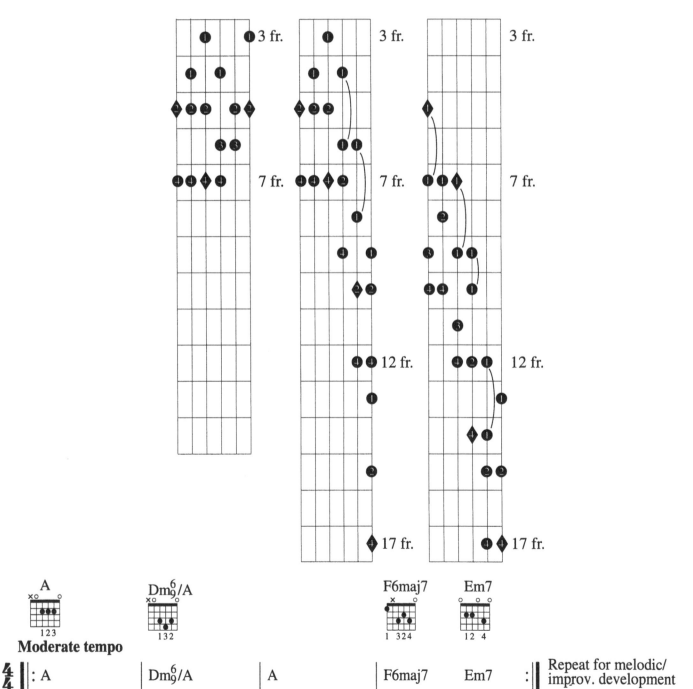

Hindu or Aeolian dominant scale: 1, 2, 3, 4, 5, ♭6, ♭7

♦ = root = slide

Moderate tempo

$\frac{4}{4}$ ‖: A | Dm⁶₉/A | A | F6maj7 Em7 :‖ Repeat for melodic/ improv. development

September '90: NATURAL-HARMONIC MAP

Did you ever wonder exactly where all the natural harmonics are? Well, I'm going to show you. What follows is a map showing where you can find natural harmonics—roots, 3rds, 5ths, ♭7ths, 9ths and even 11ths, all off one string. To produce the chime-like effect, use your fret-hand fingers to lightly touch the string over the fret area indicated. Each open string will produce the same harmonic intervals, but due to the physics behind string size, tension, and whether they are wrapped or plain, you will get different degrees of intonation. The chart shows the harmonics from the nut to the 24th fret, but there are more. From fret 24 to your bridge, the harmonic structure and layout are the reverse of fret 5 to the nut, with some extra "stuff." In other words, as you go from fret 24 towards the bridge, you will get these harmonics in this order: root, 3, 5, ♭7, root, 9, 3, ♯11, 5, 13, ♭7, 7, root, 9. The last six or seven can be difficult to pull out or even recognize, but they are there.

This harmonic map should be memorized completely. Work hard and enjoy the results! On the audio track the harmonics are played on the 3rd string.

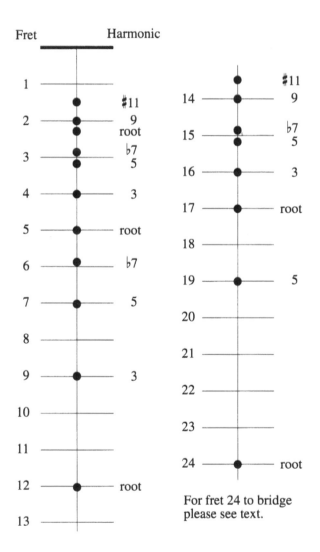

For fret 24 to bridge please see text.

36

October '90: ADVANCED IMPROVISING REVISITED

With this month's Advanced Improvising lesson, I am going to introduce you to the Gypsy scale. As with the Hindu scale, previewed in Aug. '90, the Gypsy scale has an exotic sound, due to its intervallic structure: 1, ♭2, 3, 4, 5, ♭6, 7. The chord patterns based on this scale can be equally challenging. However, the first time out should be taken easily. So to help you explore, I've written out an excerpt form a piece of mine called "Desert Sun." Use the voicings provided.

I've suggested six different melodic possibilities for the same four-bar progression. The scales are E Gypsy, E Phrygian dominant, F Lydian and E minor pentatonic blues (with additional key notes). Written out are the Gypsy and Phrygian dominant (1, ♭2, 3, 4, 5, ♭6, ♭7). You should be familiar with the Lydian and blues scales by now, but if not, check out my Photographic Memory (Parts One and Two) columns (Oct. and Nov. '89) or any other scale book you may (should!) have. Good luck!

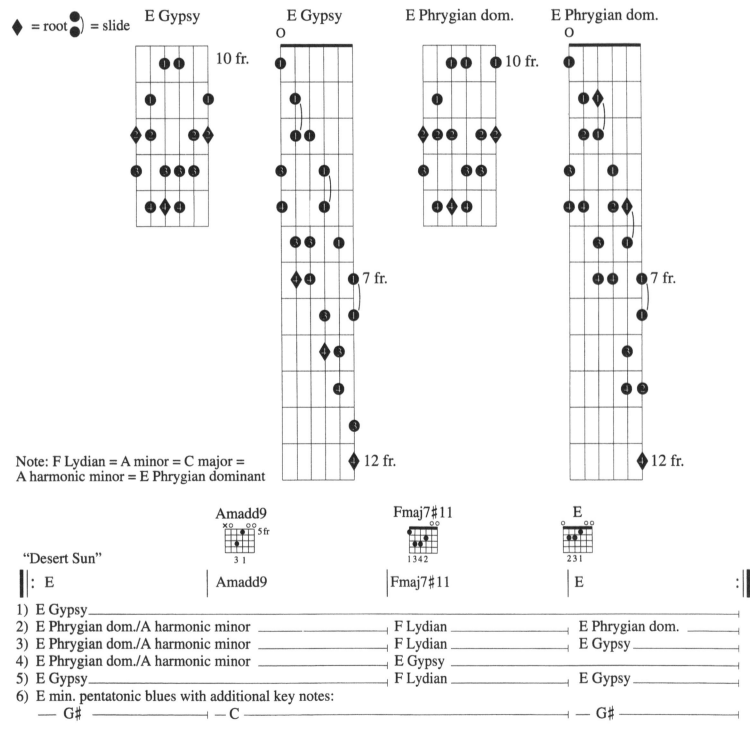

Note: F Lydian = A minor = C major =
A harmonic minor = E Phrygian dominant

"Desert Sun"

‖: E | Amadd9 | Fmaj7#11 | E :‖

1) E Gypsy
2) E Phrygian dom./A harmonic minor — F Lydian — E Phrygian dom.
3) E Phrygian dom./A harmonic minor — F Lydian — E Gypsy
4) E Phrygian dom./A harmonic minor — E Gypsy
5) E Gypsy — F Lydian — E Gypsy
6) E min. pentatonic blues with additional key notes:
— G# — C — G#

November '90: HARMONIC CRUNCH

I hate to say it, but sometimes less is more—at least when you've got to play chords with a distorted sound. Crunch tones and overdriven sound don't always go together well with traditionally fingered 6th- and 5th-string-root bar chords. Too many notes! So the key is to play only the essential tones, the ones that will not drive your overdrive nuts, but will contain the telling harmonies your song requires. The following voicings are written as 5th-string-root power chords, with E as the tonal center. By adding the open E (6th) string, you can fortify the root sound a bit more. Then by moving the 4th-string's position about the fretboard, you can create the 4th, #4th, ♭6th, 6th, ♭7th and maj7th intervals that will suggest, harmonically, the chords to be replaced. Simple, but effective. Crunch on!

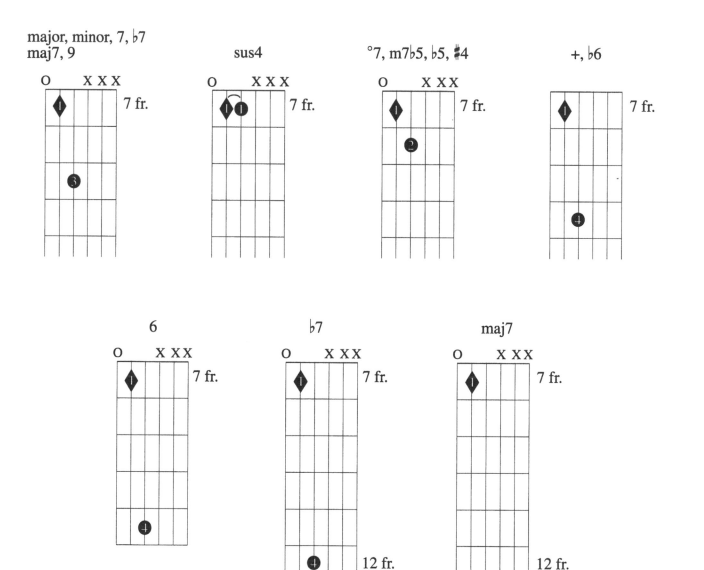

December '90: Open-String Color

Take a 6th-string-root F♯ chord and finger all but the first two strings—let them ring open. Ya know what you get? A good-sounding F♯7add4. You could also call it F♯11 (no 9th), but that's beside the point. The point is I'm going to show you how to get all sorts of chords by moving this simple fingering up and down the fretboard. By starting with a first-position E chord and moving up fret by fret, the "remaining" first two strings create some interesting and colorful harmonic tensions. So tune up and check this out!

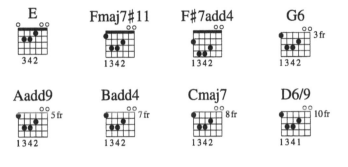

January '91: Re-Assigning Chord Intervals

One interesting way to change the key of a chord progression is not to move to a new tonal center, but to stay put and re-assign the intervals. This is sort of a pitch axis–meets–modulation compositional technique. Take a chord progression and label each chord with its key-related Roman numeral. These are the basic triad harmonizations you get when harmonizing an A major and an A minor scale with themselves:

A major:	A	Bm	C♯m	D	E	F♯m	G♯°
	I	ii	iii	IV	V	vi	vii°
A minor:	Am	B°	C	Dm	Em	F	G
	i	ii°	III	iv	v	VI	VII

Using the chord progressions shown in Ex. 1 and 2, I've taken a simple progression in A major and changed it to A minor; using the same formula from the first four bars to create the second four bars, I've simply re-harmonized the existing chords' intervals. I've reduced the chord progression to a numeric sequence and re-harmonized each chord. This is an easy way to extend a progression's life and add a "mirror image" of an existing chord sequence. Your mirror images could run consecutively (as in these examples), or the newly generated progression can be reserved for a bridge, solo section or tag. Take this idea and apply it to your own progression, however short or long. Experimentation is encouraged. Good luck.

Ex. 1

A major ―――――――――――――― A minor ――――――――――――――

4/4 A | E | D | E | Am | Em | Dm | Em ||

    I   V   IV   V   i   v   iv   v

Ex. 2

A major ―――――――――――――― A minor ――――――――――――――

4/4 A | E | F♯m | D | Am | Em | F | Dm ||

    I   V   vi   IV   i   v   VI   iv

AUDIO TRACK LISTING

Track 1: Standard Tuning Notes
Track 2: Page 4 Ex. 1
Track 3: Page 4 Ex. 2
Track 4: Page 5 Unusual Tunings
Track 5: Page 6 Right-Hand Harmonics
Track 6: Page 7 Harmonized Scales (Part One)
Track 7: Page 8 (top) Harmonized Scales (Part Two)
Track 8: Page 8 (bottom) Harmonized Scales (Part Two)
Track 9: Page 9 Ex. 1 F major
Track 10: Page 9 Ex. 1 C Dorian
Track 11: Page 9 Ex. 2 E harmonic minor
Track 12: Page 9 Ex. 2 D Phrygian dominant
Track 13: Page 10 Ex. 1
Track 14: Page 10 Ex. 2
Track 15: Page 11 F major
Track 16: Page 11 F minor
Track 17: Page 11 F diminished
Track 18: Page 11 F augmented
Track 19: Page 11 Fsus4
Track 20: Page 12 Wang 1
Track 21: Page 12 Wang 2
Track 22: Page 13
Track 23: Page 14 Ex. 1 Am11
Track 24: Page 14 Ex. 2 Amaj9♯11
Track 25: Page 14 Ex. 3 Asus4/sus2
Track 26: Page 14 Ex. 4 A11
Track 27: Page 14 Ex. 5 A7♭9
Track 28: Page 15 top
Track 29: Page 15 Lydian
Track 30: Page 15 Mixolydian
Track 31: Page 15 Dorian
Track 32: Page 15 Lydian dominant
Track 33: Page 16
Track 34: Page 17
Track 35: Page 18 C major
Track 36: Page 18 A minor
Track 37: Page 19 Ex. 1
Track 38: Page 19 Ex. 2
Track 39: Page 20
Track 40: Page 21 Ex. 1
Track 41: Page 21 Ex. 2
Track 42: Page 22 top
Track 43: Page 22 bottom
Track 44: Page 23 G major
Track 45: Page 23 A Phrygian dominant
Track 46: Page 23 bottom
Track 47: Page 24 Ionian/major
Track 48: Page 24 Dorian
Track 49: Page 24 Phrygian
Track 50: Page 24 Lydian

Track 51: Page 24 Mixolydian
Track 52: Page 24 Aeolian/minor
Track 53: Page 24 Locrian
Track 54: Page 25 Ionian/major
Track 55: Page 25 Dorian
Track 56: Page 25 Phrygian
Track 57: Page 25 Lydian
Track 58: Page 25 Mixolydian
Track 59: Page 25 Aeolian/minor
Track 60: Page 25 Locrian
Track 61: Page 26 A major
Track 62: Page 26 A minor
Track 63: Page 26 A dim.
Track 64: Page 26 A aug.
Track 65: Page 27 A(♭5)
Track 66: Page 27 Asus4
Track 67: Page 27 Asus2
Track 68: Page 28 top
Track 69: Page 28 Lydian
Track 70: Page 28 Dorian♯4
Track 71: Page 28 Hungarian
Track 72: Page 28 Symmetrical
Track 73: Page 29 Lydian
Track 74: Page 29 Dorian♯4
Track 75: Page 29 Hungarian
Track 76: Page 29 Symmetrical
Track 77: Page 30 Open D Tuning
Track 78: Page 30 Chords
Track 79: Page 31 Rhythm chords
Track 80: Page 32 E Lydian
Track 81: Page 32 G Lydian
Track 82: Page 32 B Lydian
Track 83: Page 32 E Dorian
Track 84: Page 32 B minor
Track 85: Page 33
Track 86: Page 34
Track 87: Page 35 Hindu scale 1
Track 88: Page 35 Hindu scale 2
Track 89: Page 35 Hindu scale 3
Track 90: Page 35 Chord progression
Track 91: Page 36
Track 92: Page 37 E Gypsy 1
Track 93: Page 37 E Gypsy 2
Track 94: Page 37 E Phrygian dominant 1
Track 95: Page 37 E Phrygian dominant 2
Track 96: Page 37 "Desert Sun"
Track 97: Page 38
Track 98: Page 39 top
Track 99: Page 39 bottom, Ex. 1 & 2